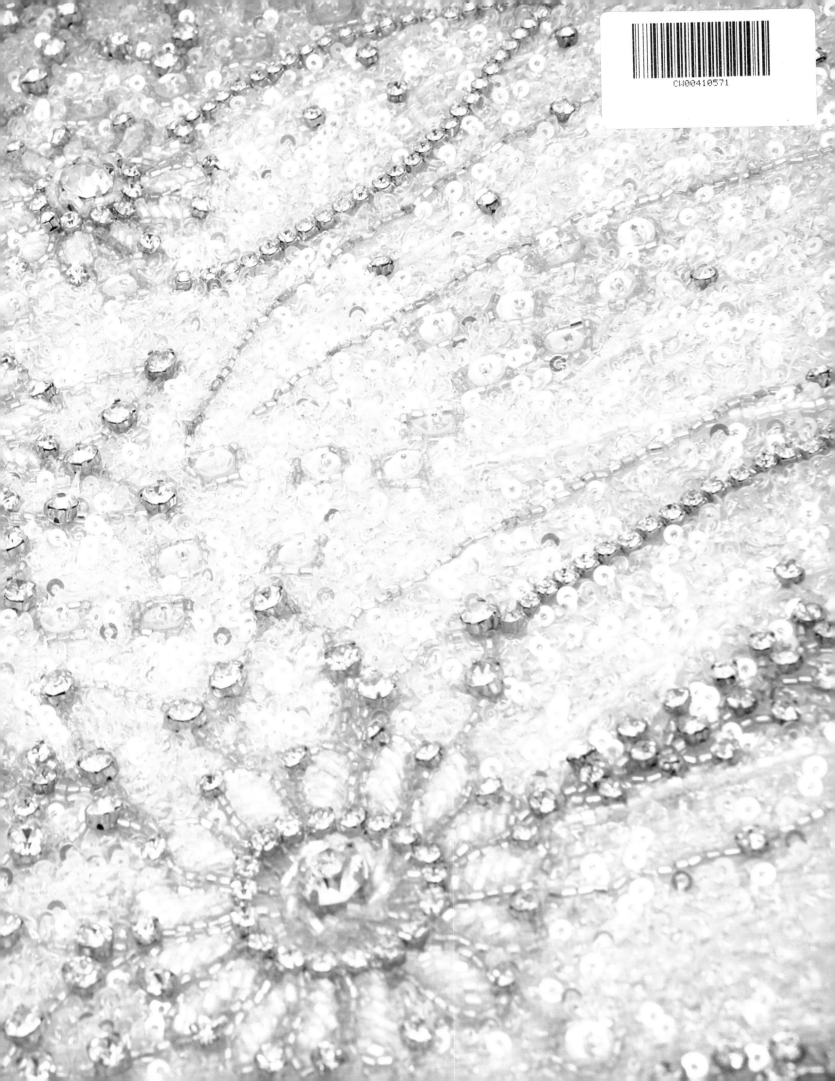

REGAL & ELEGANT

DRESSING THE QUEEN

DRESSING THE QUEEN

THE JUBILEE WARDROBE

ANGELA KELLY

I dedicate this book to

Her Majesty The Queen

to thank her for allowing the special working relationship that we have

and for the opportunity to share these special moments in this book.

Your Majesty, thank you.

Angela

I would also like to dedicate this book

to my loving family:

my eldest son, Frank Wylie and his partner, Nicola,

my second son, Paul Wylie and his lovely wife, my daughter-in-law, Sarah Wylie,

my beautiful daughter, Michelle Anson and son-in-law, Simon Anson

and especially to my four wonderful grandchildren,

James and Scarlett Anson

and the twins

Alexander and Jacob Wylie.

From the bottom of my heart I love you all so much.

Granny xxxx

The sixtieth anniversary of The Queen's accession to the throne in 1952 has given rise to a year of celebrations across the United Kingdom, the British Overseas Territories, the Realms and the Commonwealth, on a scale not seen since the last – and only other – Diamond Jubilee of a British sovereign, that of Queen Victoria in 1897.

Her Majesty The Queen has herself taken part in an exceptionally busy programme, including more than twenty-two official events and eighteen regional visits, from Leicester on 8 March to Hampshire and the Isle of Wight on 25 July, with the extraordinary weekend of 2–5 June as its centrepiece. Unlike Queen Victoria's Jubilee year, 2012 has celebrated another momentous occasion, the Olympic Games, which were officially opened by Her Majesty on 27 July.

At the heart of any Jubilee is the relationship between Sovereign and people. The presence of The Queen in a particular neighbourhood or community has a unique and indefinable magical effect, and individual and local memories are invariably formed by The Queen's appearance – her clothes. In describing the creation of The Queen's Diamond Jubilee wardrobe this book provides, for the first time, an insight into both the exceptional skill, craftsmanship and ingenuity of The Queen's dedicated Dressers, based at Buckingham Palace, and the consideration that goes into ensuring that a particular outfit suits the occasion and the locality, to say nothing of the vagaries of British weather.

Nobody is better placed to tell this hitherto unknown story than Angela Kelly, Personal Assistant, Adviser and Curator to The Queen, who for nearly twenty years has undertaken the exceptional responsibility of managing all aspects of The Queen's wardrobe with unstinting pride in her work, attention to detail and – as will be evident from this account – those vital qualities of teamwork and good humour.

I hope you will enjoy this unique celebration of a historic year.

Samantha Cohen
Assistant Private Secretary to The Queen

Introduction

When the Queen appears in public she is naturally the centre of everyone's attention; wherever she goes she looks majestic and elegant.

Have you ever wondered how she works her magic, or what lies behind her unfailing style? How is it that she is so instantly recognisable in a crowd?

Have you ever asked who designs her clothes and ensures that each outfit is perfectly completed by a unique hat? Have you ever wondered how, at the age of eighty-six, The Queen still manages to set fashion trends and maintain her individual style?

The answers to these and many more questions are revealed in this beautifully illustrated book telling you the story of The Queen and her royal wardrobe. Prepare to be amazed and amused as the fascinating story unfolds of the many months spent in planning and working to deliver this special, historic year.

Contents

An invitation

Close your eyes and imagine that you are walking through the streets of London.

You pass Big Ben, walk along The Mall, finally reaching the gates of Buckingham Palace.

Open your eyes, take a deep breath, go through the gates and walk straight to the front door.

As the footman welcomes you in, you hesitate as you see the red carpet.

As you continue further into the Palace, you realise that you are walking on the same carpet that monarchs have walked on before you.

Suddenly you get a sense of pride and honour to be in such a special place, knowing that you have just entered a part of Her Majesty's private world.

You stop.

Welcome to
The Dressers' Floor

The journey

LET me take you on an unforgettable journey into an enchanting
world of excitement and glamour that will interest and romance you.
I will help you understand the magic, dedication, inspiration and technical
expertise that underpin the design and creation of a wardrobe for
Her Majesty The Queen. I will also share with you how looking and
dressing the part helps to meet the demands of Her Majesty's everyday
life, duty and commitment. Her Majesty is not only our Queen and our
Sovereign, but also a special lady who is

Regal and Elegant

You will understand how the garments are chosen to suit the many
engagements for the Diamond Jubilee.

Step into our world, about which very little is known …
Until now.
Follow me,
Step by step,
And enter the magical world of fashion, tiaras, jewellery, millinery and
much, much more.

Join us on The Dressers' Floor within The Queen's private world, where
we can share in the sheer delight of an unforgettable experience.

Go and put the kettle on,
Make yourself a cup of tea,
Sit down, relax,
And enjoy the book.

The Dressers' Floor

THE DRESSERS' FLOOR is always an enchanting world of fashion, fabric and glamour, but this year has been exceptional in so many ways. The only other British monarch to have celebrated a Diamond Jubilee was Queen Victoria, and the world has changed a great deal since 1897. What has not changed, however, is the anticipation, the excitement and the absolute discretion surrounding the designs and planning for the all-important Jubilee wardrobe. To add to the excitement of the Jubilee, London also hosted the Olympic Games this year and The Queen, as Head of State, was invited to open them. Creating a unique wardrobe for these historic occasions has been an incredible challenge for a small team. I design the clothes and hats, and we have three dressmakers and a milliner to help cover more than three hundred engagements a year through different seasons, occasions and cultures. Our role is to ensure that Her Majesty is always dressed appropriately for the occasion, from state events to informal day wear in the United Kingdom and abroad.

I joined the Royal Household in 1994 as one of Her Majesty's Dressers. Two years later, I was honoured to be invited to become the Senior Dresser. As the years went by, The Queen created my current position: Personal Assistant, Adviser and Curator to Her Majesty, which gives me an interesting and varied portfolio to manage. This means that I am responsible for planning both The Queen's official and private wardrobes, and I am curator of Her Majesty's personal jewellery collection.

Working closely with me is an excellent team of people who provide me with the support needed to produce the perfection that The Queen's outfits demand. The Queen's Dressers are: Kate, the Deputy Dresser, who is my right-hand woman and helps manage the daily wardrobe, ensuring it is kept in pristine condition; Beverley, the Assistant Deputy Dresser; and Joanne and Timea, the Assistant Dressers. Rianna is my Personal Assistant; she handles the day-to-day running of the office, as well as helping with events and exhibitions. The Dressmakers – Emily, Desiree and Anja – work with the Milliner, Stella, to produce the intricate fashion pieces. Bernard is responsible for the beautiful illustrations of my designs in this book. Finally, Lucy and Ian came to help for a while, to cover the busy Jubilee period.

Together we have worked to create this special Diamond Jubilee wardrobe which reflects the splendour, history, ceremony and magnificence of this remarkable occasion.

Angela Kelly MVO.

A fascination with fabric

$\mathcal{I}$T ALL started when I was very young, as I was brought up surrounded by fabrics: my mother and aunt were dressmakers and taught me to sew from an early age. My mother used to make all my clothes, and when I had my own children I, too, made their clothes. So fabric has always been an important part of my life.

The preparations for the Diamond Jubilee began in earnest in 2010, when I started to research and purchase fabrics. But since The Queen is frugal and very aware of costs, I was keen to use fabrics from our stock room, some of which date back to 1961 and before. The contents of the stock room have been built up over time, from gifts that Her Majesty has received in the past on royal tours, and from purchases we have made at home and overseas. So when we started planning for the Jubilee, we already had the beginnings of an amazing collection of materials to show The Queen, including silks, jerseys, wools, sequined lace and beaded material from various locations around the British Isles and other parts of the world. Combining these with new materials, mixing old and new, seemed especially appropriate for a Diamond Jubilee collection. Not only would it reveal the inherent beauty of some of the older materials but it would be cost-effective too.

From time to time The Queen will wear the same outfit to different events, although normally several months will pass between each occasion.

It is always important to plan well ahead for all aspects of Her Majesty's calendar but, with the events of the Diamond Jubilee happening on such a large scale and across an extended period of time, it became imperative to create a couture collection suitable for Her Majesty at such an important time in her Sovereignty.

Sourcing the fabrics

Sourcing fabrics is a passion of mine, which of course means going out shopping. Selecting the right materials, colours and trimmings and accessories which are both suitable for the occasion and to The Queen's liking is both a serious responsibility and great fun. I find I still get excited when I go shopping for materials but I always let Her Majesty know too so there won't be any headaches when I return to the Palace with the bill. I am at my happiest when I know that I have all I need to produce a stunning wardrobe, and The Queen is always happy when I return before the shops have closed!

Feeling the samples

Very often I will return with large samples of materials known in the trade as 'feelers' because the size of the sample allows you to feel the texture of the fabric before deciding to buy it. As well as judging at close quarters the colour, texture and quality of the weave, I will squeeze and twist the sample around in my hands before smoothing it out once more.

If the material remains creased or crumpled, then it will be of no use and will be discarded from the selection. This is something that The Queen herself taught me: by applying this test, you can see if the material creases. I also keep a small collection of swatches of fabrics for reference and comparison as well.

On the case: Rianna ordering material

Choosing colours

Colour is one of the key criteria when choosing fabrics for Her Majesty. It is very important that the colour chosen suits not only The Queen, but also the occasion. Vibrant colours work well in the daytime and allow The Queen to stand out from the crowd during her public engagements. But as the light changes as the day wears on, or when moving from outside into candle-lit interiors, this will have an effect on the appearance of the colour and the texture of the fabric which needs to be taken into account. The Queen has to feel confident and comfortable wearing the chosen colour and the material wherever she is and whatever she is called upon to do. In essence, The Queen must always present a perfect figure at all times – quite a high standard for any fabric and design to achieve!

The enchantment

IN the world of fashion, the majority of designers produce collections twice a year to cater for two broad time spans – spring/summer and autumn/winter. However, for Her Majesty, each of the four seasons is equally important and must therefore be considered separately and individually. And, of course, if The Queen is travelling overseas, then the seasons are going to be different and the prevailing weather conditions of each country need to be considered. But to make things simpler, let's just consider the familiar seasons of our own climate, here in the United Kingdom, and how their colours and climates can set my imagination free when designing and planning outfits appropriate to the locations to be visited within The Queen's public engagement schedule.

Spring brings bright yellow daffodils, crisp bluebells, the pink blush of cherry blossom, clean white lily of the valley, fresh lemon primroses and beautiful creamy magnolias, each set fair against pale blue skies and surrounded by luminous, verdant green. This season inspires me to introduce delicate, paler colours into The Queen's wardrobe, and silk dresses with spring flower motifs. Lightweight coats and jackets make an entrance, with similarly lightweight fabric hats, adorned with crystals to twinkle and flash in the bright spring sunshine. However, spring is a changeable season in Britain, so I must also ensure that warmer fabrics are used to shield Her Majesty from the chill winds of March, April showers and May's light winds.

Summer arrives in June, and we always hope for long days of golden sunshine and azure blue skies, and lingering evenings of gathering violet dusk. If we are lucky with the weather, the whole countryside comes to life in a sea of colour that inspires every aspect of my designs: the deep blue of delphiniums, sweet purple lilacs, jade and sage green foliage and riotous yellow roses. This season calls for light and

of the seasons

dynamic fabrics that can move and flow with the warm summer breezes. Strong floral patterns work well with both vibrant colours and pastel shades, while luxurious silk linings of bright colours add contrast and highlight a cool, summer feel. Hats are individually made, each conceived and produced to co-ordinate with an individual outfit, and will be constructed from light Sinamay straws, adorned with crystals or feathers or summer flowers to come alive in the sparkling sunshine.

Autumn introduces cooler weather once again from early September, but with this comes a magnificent change of colour palette too. This season brings the mellowness of ripe fruits and the reddening leaves as they begin to change and fall from the trees. Russet reds, bronze and copper, with ochre earths, blue-black plum and dark greens all come together to create the unmistakable colours of autumn. With falling temperatures we introduce medium to heavier

weighted fabrics, utilising wools, cashmere, double crêpes and bouclé in anticipation of a brisk wind or a cold day. Her Majesty's outfits take their inspiration from this autumnal spectrum and will feature sumptuous colours in warmer woven checks and mixed texture fabrics.

Winter brings the close of the year and the harshest of weathers, but in our minds this is the season of dazzling white snow and glittering silvery frost, adorned with vivid red berries, the shiny dark green leaves of the holly and, of course, the beautiful silver-olive of mistletoe with its pale ivory berries. Against this background The Queen's colour palette is one of antique gold, royal blue, deep purple and rich claret. I am inspired to design with silky velvets, soft cashmeres and heavier wools, using larger collars, matching scarves and warm hats with trims. Whatever the weather, The Queen will continue with her royal responsibilities looking elegant and poised in outfits that are comfortable and stylish.

Fabric comes first

SOME designers can visualise a design for an outfit in their minds, translate their vision to paper with a sketch and there you have it – a 'creation'. But there are also designers who get their inspiration from seeing and touching materials and this is the way that it works for me.

I like to find a quiet moment – often at the end of the day – when I can hide away in the materials room and play with the fabrics, using my imagination and allowing them to shape themselves into a design.

With soft, light material I look for lots of movement, watching to see if the flow is graceful and elegant. Occasionally I might even switch on a fan to move the air around, just to see how the fabric moves in the breeze, especially with dynamic, floating and weightless fabrics such as chiffon, organza, silk or crêpe de chine.

Studying the materials in this way sets my imagination alight; fabrics really do inspire me to create designs and make ideas come to life.

I will normally try to imagine and sketch at least four different designs for a particular piece of fabric, giving The Queen a choice. But if it's a fabric that I really like, I can produce many more designs for that specific material. It then becomes a dilemma of decision-making – bearing in mind that the world's eye is on Her Majesty, each individual outfit must be different.

The Queen's wardrobe must be one of the most wide-ranging and considered in the world. Royal outfits can vary so much, from a simple but elegant day dress to a formal and highly finished state gown.

The Queen has a fantastic understanding of clothes and fashion and is very aware of what suits her and what would be appropriate for any occasion. We will review the designs to ensure that they convey a chic and elegant style. We also prepare a range of design sketches and attach swatches of the chosen materials to each, so that The Queen can envisage what is intended for the outfit.

After our initial discussion on any given outfit, I will make a note of The Queen's wishes and ideas for changes and alterations. I will then finalise the design and produce a technical drawing for the pattern to be cut. I will discuss the design pattern and material with the dressmakers to enable them to take the outfit to the fitting stage.

Bernard and I going through the
illustrations for this book

Alone with my designs

Appropriate for the occasion

MANY of The Queen's outfits are created for specific events, such as when Her Majesty and His Royal Highness The Duke of Edinburgh travel overseas on a royal tour or for a state visit, or when members of other royal families or heads of state visit Britain and are welcomed by The Queen. On these occasions The Queen and I will review the designs to try to find a style that will be sympathetic to the visitors' culture and country.

An example of The Queen's consideration for her hosts or guests was the visit she made to the Republic of Ireland in May 2011, the first time a British monarch had visited the Republic. As a sign of respect for Ireland and her long-held affection for the country, The Queen chose to wear a day outfit that was predominantly green in colour. For the evening gown for the state banquet in Dublin Castle on 18 May 2011 she was very specific in her guidance to me: the gown featured more than two thousand silk shamrocks especially designed for the dress and sewn on by hand. This work, undertaken by Tina, our expert beadier, was intricate and painstaking but was just what we needed to bring the gown to life. We then created an Irish harp design, made up of crystals, to be worn on The Queen's left shoulder, where on state occasions she would normally wear a Royal Family Order. This collaboration of design, dressmaking skills and cultural empathy was deeply appreciated and met with great approval from all.

The Queen on her visit to the Republic of Ireland in 2011

Keeping a record

We often like to give names to The Queen's outfits and coming up with the names can be a lot of fun; it also makes it easier for our own reference purposes. When putting together a wardrobe around a royal schedule, it is vital to consult our detailed records of what The Queen has worn before. For example, if Her Majesty wore red when she last visited the south of England we would avoid using red again – even if the design was completely different. This is because it is the colour that gives the predominant impression – especially on television – so it could look too similar to the one previously worn.

To keep a track of this, all the dressers keep their own individual wardrobe diaries, recording the details of each outfit and the events at which it was worn, which is where we have fun inventing appropriate names. Each dresser keeps her own separate handwritten record so that if one were to get lost or damaged, there are others that will survive as a back-up. By cross-checking the wardrobe diaries, Kate, the Deputy Dresser, and the Dressers' Team are always able correctly to identify which outfits and colours were worn for which events, thus enabling a rotation to be implemented. The wardrobe diaries also record the wearing of significant jewellery, as The Queen's jewellery collection is extensive, and thus are useful for future reference.

Creating the designs

All designs by Angela Kelly

Angela Kelly M.V.O.

Sensitivity to detail

WHEN making up an outfit for The Queen, I continually draw on the feedback that I have received from Her Majesty during our design meetings and fitting sessions over the years. Here are some examples of the sorts of details that I think about to ensure that The Queen looks good and feels comfortable in a garment that is well made and a perfect fit.

Necklines on coats and jackets are very important as they must not be too high or too low and they must not restrict The Queen's movement in any way, especially when getting in and out of vehicles. This is especially true of thick wool coats with wide, full collars. The neckline shape is carefully considered in the context of the overall design – for example, whether a round, oval or sweetheart neckline looks best with which dress. A low neckline on a long dress allows a distinctive necklace to sit very well and be seen. A square or V-neck can also be deployed, but this will rule out wearing a large necklace, so a drop diamond or a single string of pearls or diamonds might be chosen instead. In warmer weather I typically design with a more open neckline, while in cold weather the neckline will be higher and closed up for warmth and comfort.

Bouclé wool is a gorgeous soft and warm fabric with a curly looped surface that reminds me of tightly curled lamb's wool. It is perfect for making a winter coat, but we have to pay attention to the sleeve area as the small loops that make up its unique texture can easily pull and catch on objects, such as the winder on The Queen's watch. We also have to be careful with loose-woven wools, as they can easily lose their shape; they require a good lining to avoid losing their shape. Loose-weave fabrics can also develop loose strands, making them appear unkempt and unattractive. I constantly have to ask myself questions such as 'will this material fold and hang nicely or will it fray?'

When The Queen is travelling in a car and sitting down for long periods of time, her coat or jacket must be comfortable and practical. Here is where non-crease fabrics come into their own. The Queen must be confident when she steps out of a vehicle that her outfit will fall correctly and not crumple; the same applies to any outfit, even long evening gowns. This means that chiffon, for example, while being a beautiful fabric also has drawbacks that have to be taken into consideration when designing an outfit. Too much fabric in a long evening dress can also make it difficult when getting in and out of cars, and large, heavy beading on a gown can make for an uncomfortable time, especially on the back or when sitting down! Nonetheless, The Queen understands that beading and crystal work are sometimes necessary to produce a spectacular effect and so does not mind some discomfort when looking the part is important.

The lengths of dresses will vary according to the occasion. Daywear is usually designed to stop just below the knee, whereas a cocktail dress for a drinks reception could be just below the knee or ballerina length, finishing just on or below the bottom of the calf. This length is particularly good as it enables Her Majesty to walk unhindered. Stairs can also present a problem for dresses if they are too long or too tight. This is why, on occasions, you will see The Queen wearing a straight dress that incorporates a split to the front, back or side of the skirt, or different kinds of pleat – knife, box and kick pleats are all used. You will also see The Queen wearing skirts that flare out from a fitted hip or knee as these allow for easy movement. We will often use a fishtail in long skirts as this gives a lovely shape to the back while still allowing for movement.

Overall, The Queen likes her clothes to be fitted but not too tight, with a sleeve length of either three-quarters or full – definitely not too wide or full at the wrists as this could be awkward at the dining table – after all, we don't want the cuffs ending up in the soup, do we?

Glamour at its best

As you can see, this evening dress with a wrapover front is made from heavily beaded silver mesh lace, with crystal diamanté forming a series of parallel lines. It would have been easy to run the lines horizontally or vertically, but such a wonderful material demands a more creative approach, so I decided to cut on the bias to create a chevron pattern. The result is a flattering shape moulded to the body that is easy to walk in and that harks back to the glamorous styles worn by 1930s movie stars. I was also inspired by The Queen Mother's dresses of the time. I picked the bow as the perfect detail to finish the outfit. I hope you like it – look out for The Queen wearing this beautiful evening dress on engagements in the future.

From fabric to couture

ONCE the fabric and the design sketch have been approved by The Queen, the next step is to produce a technical drawing that will be used to make the pattern and will also help to brief the dressmakers and hatmaker.

Cutting a pattern is a highly skilled task, requiring both technical knowledge and common sense. The dressmakers' team is well experienced in this field, knowing the shape of the human body, the ways that different fabrics behave and how the overall design should flow. The patterncutter translates this into flat panels of paper or card, collectively known as 'the block',

and the block is used to cut out the various pieces of fabric required for the whole outfit.

Once the material is cut to the pattern, the outfit starts to take shape. When cutting fabric you must bear in mind the matching of any dyed or printed patterns or floral motifs on the fabric, as nothing looks worse than a flower being cut in half by a seam. Once the fabric has been cut and pinned on to the mannequin, the dressmaker is briefed on the making of the whole outfit, including buttons, trimmings, collars, cuffs and any patterns that need to be matched on the seams.

'Amongst the heather'

Sometimes I will ask the dressmaker to make a prototype version of the garment before we start cutting up the fabric from which the final garment will be made. The prototype is called a *toile* in the tailoring trade. *Toile* is a French word for 'linen' or 'canvas', used in this context to refer to a test garment that is made from calico, a rough cotton, so that we can work out the fine detail of a technically difficult design. This is especially important when working with very expensive fabrics. Once the calico for the *toile* has been cut out and tacked together, it is fitted on to a mannequin and adjusted to reflect The Queen's exact size and body shape. By doing this first, we can make adjustments to the shape and length of the sleeves, necklines, skirts and hems before finally cutting the fabric itself. Design details and instructions for the making-up itself can be written on to the *toile* in pencil, giving very clear and concise instructions to the dressmaker.

We follow a similar process for hats but we use straw instead of calico to make a prototype. We have many millinery blocks, to create the different shapes of hat designs, and we follow the same making-up procedure as for outfits, getting every last detail finalised on the straw prototype before moving on to the real thing. But more about hats later.

The making of 'Amongst the heather'

Fitting and finishing

Fitting sessions with The Queen can typically last half a day, though, sometimes, if we just have one or two important outfits to try on, The Queen will set aside a shorter time for this in the mornings. I try to ensure that we have at least four or five outfits ready to be fitted at any one session to make the best use of Her Majesty's time. The dressmaker who is making up the garments will be present, with her trusted tools – a wooden measuring stick, a small pair of

scissors, a tape measure, pincushion or pin tin and tailor's chalk. Often, we are joined by one or two of The Queen's corgis, who like to keep a watchful canine eye on things! Otherwise, as with any fitting session, these are very private and we are the only people present.

We try to make the fitting sessions relaxing and enjoyable for The Queen. On those occasions when a *toile* has been made, it will be fitted on Her Majesty so that I can make sure that she is happy with the shape, length, style and fit of the outfit. This also gives the dressmaker a second

chance to write up any adjustments, for example, changing the style of a pocket, a neckline or a collar.

When a *toile* is not required, the outfit will have been tacked together by the dressmaker, so it can easily be adjusted, if necessary, after the fitting session. The same is true for our hats, which we always include in the fittings, to check the overall look. It is, of course, The Queen's prerogative to have second thoughts and to change her mind about an outfit that she has previously seen as a sketch or as a length of fabric draped over a mannequin. It has to be said that Her Majesty's instincts are usually correct, however: she normally stays with her first choice, rarely changing her mind.

This made it much easier to agree the intricacies of the designs and type of fabrics that would be used for the all-important Diamond Jubilee Collection. We expected to have to set aside additional time for further fittings, which would have provided a challenge, since Her Majesty's diary is even fuller this year than most. However, The Queen's decisiveness and the way my team worked so well together, with such a close eye on the detail, meant that we were able to complete a record number of outfits in a relatively short space of time.

The Queen will next see the finished garments and hats a day or so before the commencement of a royal tour or engagement, trying them on just to check that the entire outfit is to her complete satisfaction. On the actual day itself, Kate, Beverley and I will prepare the outfit and a choice of brooches to complement it. We will lay these out with a handbag, gloves, headscarf and shoes, all ready for The Queen to dress for her engagement. Normally in the daytime, a hat will be part of the outfit and so we will always provide a matching headscarf, just in case the hat gets wet and is damaged in the rain. We also always ensure that The Queen has a transparent umbrella (so that everyone can still see her), with a coloured handle and edged trim co-ordinated to match the colour of her outfit. For those rare sunny days we will provide a parasol for shade.

Many hands make light work

Standing out and fitting in

THE QUEEN is very conscious that she must be seen when she is out and about and so we will always choose striking colours for her outfits, so that she will stand out from the rainbow of shades worn by the crowd of wellwishers. The Queen is always concerned that she can be seen from as far away as possible and is also very aware of the intensive media coverage that her presence will attract. Nonetheless, some occasions are too solemn or poignant for bright colours, so we face the challenge of retaining a degree of prominence with colours that are appropriate to the occasion. We also have to consider the circumstances and surroundings in which The Queen will be seen – if she is going to plant a tree in a situation with a predominantly green background, the last colour we need to choose is another green!

The Queen is aware that colours have all sorts of symbolic associations and that they can also reflect a variety of emotions – happiness, condolence or respect, for example. So helping The Queen put across her desired message by selecting the right colour and outfit gives me real satisfaction. And working with such a wide palette of colours and shades gives me pleasure too.

For example, when The Queen visits a school or a children's centre, we make sure she is dressed in a bright, jolly colour and that her hat has the kind of details that will appeal to children. We will use feathers, twirls, twists, flowers and ribbons – all these will help to keep children occupied and hold their attention, especially if they are very young. There are other practical considerations to be taken into account when designing and selecting specific outfits for specific occasions. For example, when visiting a nursing or a residential home for older people, The Queen prefers to wear a strong, well-defined colour with a well-structured hat, to help those who are visually impaired to see her and feel part of the visit.

When planning a hat for The Queen, I will naturally take into consideration the design and colour of the outfit, but the size of the crown and brim are also important if the occasion includes a walkabout. The Queen is very aware that people travel from far and wide hoping to get a glimpse of her, so visibility is always an important factor. On such occasions, she is likely to wear a hat with a fair-sized crown, not only to give her height but also to enable young and old to see her.

Glitter and glamour

OUTFITS for formal engagements often require a little bit of shine and sparkle. And every designer knows that beading, sequins and crystals can transform an otherwise flat fabric. For me and my team there is nothing so special as a Diamond Jubilee year, and we were inspired to create some really memorable outfits for this historic celebration!

Beads, crystals and sequins come in all shapes and sizes. They are sourced from many of the places that we have visited on the royal tours, as I take the opportunity to purchase fine-quality, locally made fabrics and trimmings wherever we go. We will consider ready-beaded material

too, but there are many questions to be considered first, since cutting through beaded material can be a nightmare. We do it by using a small hammer to smash the beads along the lines you are going to sew – especially along the seams – so as to make room for the machine stitching.

And while large beads may look dramatic, they can be very uncomfortable, particularly if you are required to sit down on them! We have found that it helps to have a few extra layers of lining under the top layer of material to help cushion the impact, especially at the back of the dress. We also keep large heavily beaded areas to the front and sides, with finer beads to the back, below the zip area. Larger beads can also be added to the hemlines or lower areas to balance the overall weight of the dress.

Angela Kelly MVO

When thinking about embellishments, such as beads and crystals, you also have to consider the main fabric on to which they will be mounted. For glamorous formal occasions this can often mean a lightweight wool or Shantung silk, crêpe or lace, or another fine fabric. How will they hold up under the weight and pull of beading or sequins? Additional beads or crystals must therefore match the fabric, and these adornments will be handsewn on to the gown by whichever of our dressmakers has the necessary magic touch for such detailed work. Perfect eyesight is a big help – especially when you are trying to thread such small beads! It can take many days of detailed and painstaking work to achieve the desired finish but the key benefit of this couture approach is that it results in an outfit that is truly unique.

The inspiration of tradition

During the royal tour of Canada that took place in 2010, The Queen was delighted to meet people from the indigenous Mi'kmaq community. The 'People of the Dawn', as they are called, are famous for their intricate beading work, among other things, so, during the initial reconnaissance, when the details of the tour were being discussed, we had the honour of meeting the Chiefs of the Mi'kmaq nation. In recognition of their unique beading skills, I asked the Chiefs if the oldest generation of skilled women would like to embellish the yellow jacket that I had planned for The Queen to wear on the occasion of her visit.

This was a very unusual suggestion, since The Queen's outfits are normally kept secret for maximum impact on the day, but I felt it was the right decision, as their knowledge of beading goes back hundreds of years. When we got back to London after the 'recce', we produced a pattern for the collar and cuffs of the jacket that The Queen would wear and sent the fabric to the Mi'kmaq beading team. They took enormous pride in being asked to undertake this work, and returned it to us quickly for the final making-up. It really made the outfit special and was a lovely gesture done in such a personal way that gave added meaning to the outfit that The Queen wore when she made her official visit.

The Queen visiting a Mi'kmaq community during her tour of Canada in 2010

From start to finish

After 6pm The Queen does not usually wear a hat but may wear a headpiece, and to the evening state banquets, a tiara

Buttons and zips

You might think of buttons as something very practical, but we like to think of them as an opportunity for creative embellishment. Buttons come in an even greater variety of patterns, colours and styles than beads and jewels. And as if there isn't enough choice already, we can even make our own buttons by covering them using a fabric chosen to complement or harmonise with the garment we are designing. This will also make the finished effect unique.

Buttons can be very important enhancements to an outfit or they can be a mystery, hidden away behind a panel of fabric – a placket – so as to take nothing away from the detail of the design and the quality of the fabric. They can match the colour of the fabric or be made to be a contrast, so deciding on their role within a design is important. We also make buttonholes very carefully, with a combination of hand stitching and fine machine stitching to frame the buttonhole. On occasion we might even frame the hole with another fabric, or we might go further still and use frogging (ornamental braiding) as a major feature of the design, to complement embroidery or beading. For heavy coats it is vital to get the buttons into their precise positions, otherwise the coat will not sit straight on the body.

But there are also many other ways of fastening an outfit discreetly: we use large and small poppers and a whole variety of coloured and concealed zips and fasteners. Zips are a fabulous invention that come into their own especially when The Queen has to attend a large number of engagements in a given day. This means several changes of outfit, and if you want to make clothing easy to put on, then go for zips every time. It is much more convenient for The Queen to be able to step

in and out of a dress that we can zip or unzip. Trying to lift a garment over the head can wreak havoc with hair, as all ladies know. Neither do you want to get make-up on your outfit – when wearing a black or white dress, or any pale colour, this can be disastrous.

Finally, a word about the discreet use of weights in hemlines. The Queen undertakes a wide range of engagements, many of which take place in the open air, where a sudden breeze could cause embarrassment. If we think this is a possibility, we will very occasionally use weights, discreetly sewn into the seams of day dresses. That way we can ensure that The Queen will always be poised and elegant, whatever the weather.

Even the back should sparkle!

53

What a difference a hat makes!

GETTING The Queen's hat right is every bit as important as the main outfit, and we start to think about how the two will work together as soon as the fabric has been chosen and the design for the outfit begins to take shape. Here I work closely with Stella, the milliner, to envisage what sort of contribution we want the hat to make to the overall look of the finished outfit. I will probably already have had a discussion with The Queen about the shapes that would work best with the various outfit designs that have been selected.

If not, we will look at the different hat blocks and shapes that we know from experience will suit The Queen and will work for her in varying engagements, remembering at all times the practicalities of wearing and moving around in a hat. The brim should not be too large or too small, as The Queen must be able to see in all directions and be seen from all angles. The crown can be higher and sharply angled so that everyone can easily see Her Majesty, but not so high as to cause a problem getting in and out of cars. And the back of the hat must not be too long so that it catches on the collar of her coat and pushes forward on her head.

We will also look at a range of colours that will help the milliner create a hat that will make a totally distinctive impression but also complement the fabric of the outfit. Sometimes we will make use of some of the fabric from which the dress or the coat is being made, usually deploying this on the crown or brim of the hat. Almost always we will use feathers and trimmings, and we like to make our own decorative flowers from satin, silk, organza or chiffon. These beautiful materials are also perfect for draping and fixing around the hat.

Tools of the trade

$\mathcal{H}$ATS are seasonal, just like the rest of The Queen's clothes, and we use different materials for the hats, depending on the weather. In summer, Sinamay straw is a popular choice as it is light and airy, designed to keep one's head cool. In spring or autumn, fabric-covered shapes or heavier straws are used, such as buckram, millinery canvas, parasisal or parabuntal straw. These materials are warmer and better suit the heavier fabrics used for The Queen's outfits during the seasons when the weather is a little fresher. And when winter arrives, the hats become fully fabric-covered in heavier weights of materials, such as felt or wool.

But it is not just the seasons that dictate the design and composition of The Queen's hats. The occasion itself may bring its own demands. For Royal Ascot, The Queen's hats have a lighter feel, with sophisticated designs, not only because the race meeting is always held in mid-June but because it is famous as an opportunity for the milliner's art and craft to be seen and appreciated! At the other end of the fashion scale, a sturdier hat, for country pursuits, would be in keeping for attending church services in Scotland and the annual Braemar Royal Highland Gathering, held at the beginning of September.

Start of something new

Making any hat is challenging, but making a couture hat even more so. Stella and I put a lot of time and thought into those personal details that make The Queen's hats unique, knowing that they have to be perfect and very special, as the whole world will be watching.

Most of the materials we use are based on plant fibres. Sinamay straw, for example, is a natural fibre from the banana plant grown in the Philippines. The Sinamay weave is made from a coarse fibre which, when untreated, is like a thick grass but which when split to make the fibres finer can be woven like a traditional fabric. It is an ideal material for hats as it is light and porous, to allow air to move through it, but it can be sculpted and manipulated into shapes, including loops and bows. It can also be stiffened and dyed in amazing colours to match any outfit. Before hatmakers discovered its versatility, finely woven Sinamay was very popular with flower arrangers.

You can see from the pictures opposite how the feathers have been dyed, and Ian is now cutting them into the required shape.

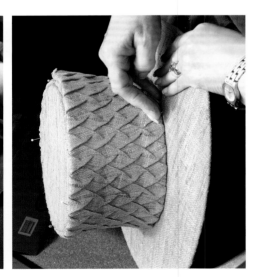

Winter warmth

FOR the autumn and winter seasons, we mainly use felts to create and mould The Queen's hats. Some of the felts have exotic names, such as Antelope, Velour, Peach Bloom, Soleil and Mellusine. They all have different 'hair' lengths – varying depths of felt pile – and each gives the finished hat a different look. Most commonly we use Velour or Peach Bloom felts, as these have a fine fur surface which gives a clean yet soft finish.

Felt is a wonderful non-woven fabric that is held together by 'barbs' that occur naturally in wool or hair fibres. These microscopic hooks can be opened with the aid of heat and moisture, allowing the felt to be manipulated before the barbs close up again, to solidify the shape. Felt can be stretched in all directions and is 'blocked' by pulling it over wooden shapes using lots of steam. Blocks come in two shapes: a cone, which is used for the crown of the hat, and a capelin, which is used to create the brim. When we are

making a felt hat, first the felt is stiffened. A spirit-based stiffener is brushed over the surface of the material in circular motions and the selected wooden blocks of crown and brim are covered with cling film.

Then the blocking of the hat begins. The felt itself is lightly sprayed with water and placed over a steamer nozzle, turning it often to allow the steam to permeate fully and evenly throughout the material. The felt hood is left over the steam until there is a fine, dew-like layer all over the surface. Then, while still hot, the steaming felt is pulled over the wooden block, stretched and turned while an even pressure is kept, until the shape is fully covered. It is then pinned in place and allowed to cool and dry out. As the fibres cool they settle into place, taking the shape of the hat block.

Once dry, the crown and the brim can be tacked together and we can begin to think about the trim. Petersham ribbon is used to create the headband and this is stitched in using tiny but firm invisible stitches. Hats can be trimmed with crystals, feathers or spines, which work as a lovely strong contrast to the matt surface of the felt. Artificial flowers can also be made from felt and other fabrics, but during the winter weather we must be careful with feathers, especially the longer ones

such as ostrich and pheasant, as they move in the wind and can go limp in the rain. Short feathers such as duck, goose and turkey are far more resilient and hold their shape well when stitched down. Once we have gone through the alternative shapes and colours of fabrics, feathers and trimmings, Stella will make up a sample of the proposed hat for The Queen to view. Then a fitting is arranged with The Queen, during which she will decide if she requires any alterations to the hat. Only when The Queen has tried on the hat alongside the outfit and is satisfied will Stella go ahead and complete the hat with all the finishing touches.

Finally, The Queen's hats would not be complete without the hat pins. We have hat pins for each hat and they are custom-made to complement the hat. We keep the hat pins in the hats to keep them safe.

The Queen also has a small selection of feature hat pins, made of gold or decorated with diamonds and moonstones. Unlike Queen Mary, her grandmother, who had a vast collection of hat pins, The Queen prefers to use her favourite pieces regularly. Interestingly, Queen Mary regarded her hat pins as a key part of her wardrobe. In those days, the ladies wore large, wide-brimmed hats and also wore their long hair up and so needed very long hat pins – and lots of them!

Hats, hats and more hats

All designs by Angela Kelly

Accessories with style

THE QUEEN's shoes are mostly made by hand and in many different styles; what they all have in common is a high degree of comfort. When you think about how much time The Queen spends on her feet during her many visits and walkabouts to meet the public, or standing to watch celebratory performances or to give speeches, you will appreciate why a comfortable heel height is essential.

For formal dinners and state occasions, The Queen will wear more elegant evening shoes, usually featuring a T-bar or a silk bow. No matter what type of shoe she wears, The Queen favours a two-inch heel, though for uneven surfaces, such as cobbles, gravel or grass, she will wear shoes with a much flatter heel.

Most of The Queen's handbags are also custom-made. A classic black patent bag is often used for a day function, while smaller, more elegant bags are used for dinners and formal events. For special occasions The Queen may also carry a special bag designed to match her outfit, and this may feature beads and crystals. The weight of a handbag is very important – in fact it is vital, given that The Queen may have to carry it for some time. She likes longer handles, so that her handbags hang from her forearm without catching on her cuffs.

Gloves and scarves

The Queen is famous for her gloves, from elegant evening gloves to the shorter pairs she wears during the daytime. We keep a large selection of day gloves which come in colours to complement her outfits while also matching her shoes. The gloves are made of pure cotton jersey. This is a high-quality fabric with a small amount of stretch, to make them comfortable to wear, and a high percentage of cotton to allow the hand to breathe inside. For the evening, elegant three-quarter-length gloves are worn to the elbow.

Her Majesty also likes her handkerchiefs and she has a wide selection in various sizes, colours and trims. For normal daytime use we lay out a plain white with a motif. For afternoon tea, a slightly smaller hanky is appropriate, while for walking and country pursuits, we lay out medium-sized tartan or checks.

The Queen has always worn headscarves for the country, and especially for riding. Shown here are just some of the wide range of scarves available for all occasions, to match whatever outfit The Queen is wearing.

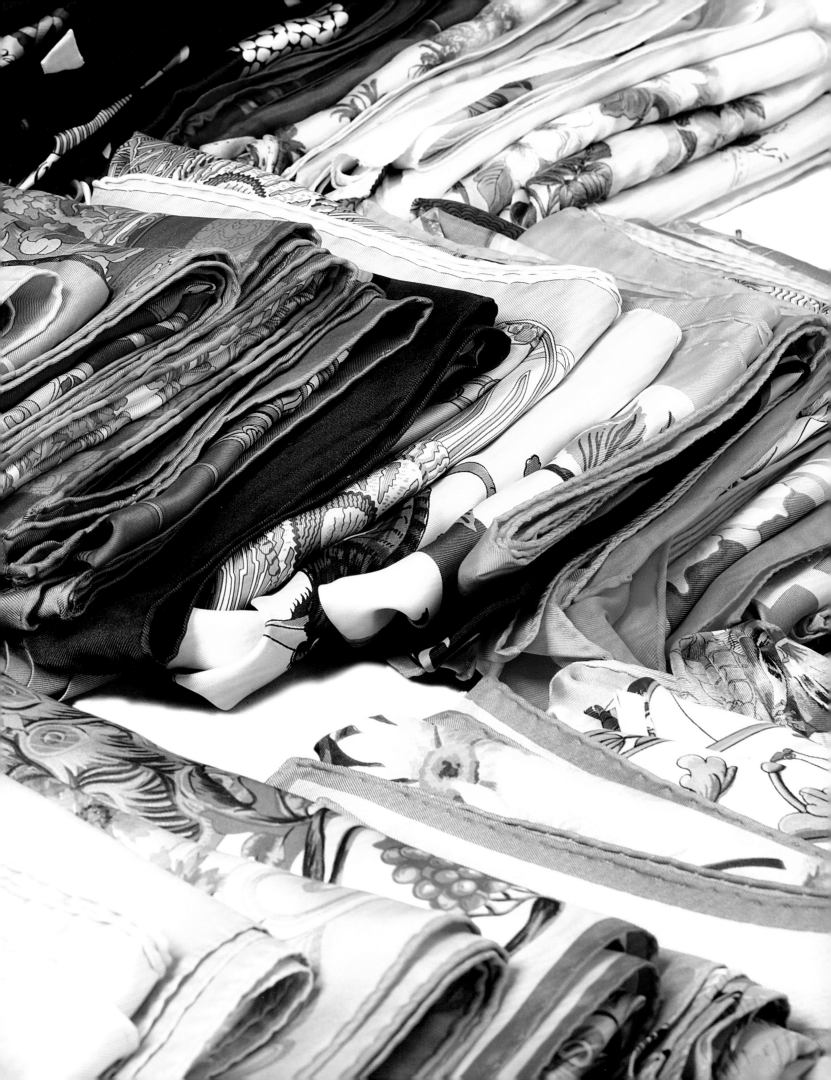

Handkerchiefs for all occasions

Umbrellas

It goes without saying that a good stock of umbrellas is a necessity for the British monarch! For many years The Queen has used a particular transparent model which ensures that even in the wettest conditions she remains as visible as possible. The umbrellas come in every possible colour so as to match whatever she is wearing.

Taking care of The Queen's wardrobe

OUR MOTTO is 'be prepared', as one of our key duties is to ensure that The Queen's outfits are in pristine condition and ready to be worn at any time and at a moment's notice.

This means all outfits are carefully inspected every time they are worn. All these functions are organised or undertaken by the dressers, who will steam and iron the garments to remove creases, and spot clean, dry clean or launder as necessary. Minor repairs, such as a hem alteration or the securing of a loose button, will be carried out by The Queen's dressers. More advanced repairs are handed over to the dressmakers, but outfits that we did not make ourselves may be returned for repair by their original designers.

Once an outfit has been prepared for wearing, we enclose it in a clear plastic bag (similar to dry-cleaning bags), ready to be hung in the wardrobes. In the case of heavily beaded gowns, we lay them out flat in large, shallow drawers. Velvets are stored in cotton covers, as plastic can make the fabric sweat. Older evening gowns will be packed in black tissue paper to protect silver or gold thread from becoming tarnished.

Thank goodness we have moved on from the old irons!

Hats require very little maintenance and Stella, the milliner, can handle whatever alterations or repairs are required. Hats are stored, with their hat pins, on a hat stand, in the wardrobes underneath the original outfits for which they are made; for travelling they are placed in large, protective hat boxes.

Handkerchiefs and scarves are always laundered by the dressers. Shoes and bags can require polishing, which is typically done by The Queen's Footmen, Ian and William. New shoes can sometimes be stretched to be made more comfortable, for which we have a range of wooden shoe stretchers.

Going on tour

S O WITH all the outfits created and the shoes, gloves and handbags ready, we set about preparing for a tour by talking through all the events that are going to take place and making sure that everyone understands the significance of each occasion. This may also involve being briefed on the precise travelling arrangements, because often The Queen is expected to undertake an event immediately after stepping off the train or the aeroplane.

Each event will be discussed in detail, so that everyone in the team knows which outfits are being worn on which occasion, and to ensure that all aspects have been considered fully for each event, including any rest days. And although I have laid great emphasis on the way that we design a specific outfit for a given event, we also have other options available, to ensure that The Queen always has a choice on the day.

At this point we also request all the royal luggage to be prepared by The Queen's Footmen. This is delivered to the Dressers' Floor so that we can start packing. The luggage comes in different sizes – large and small, wide and long – and each piece has a specific use and an important role to play. For example, we always use a large suitcase for transporting handbags and we always pack the insides with tissue to ensure that they keep their shape and do not get crushed. Last year I went shopping again, this time to buy new lightweight luggage with wheels, much to the delight of The Queen's Footmen, as they have proved to be highly practical.

THE QUEEN

The outfits are hung on rails and the hats laid on shelves in the sequence that the events themselves will take place, including different options depending on the weather and changes of clothes for travelling in comfort. Once all the outfits are arranged, they are packed in the same sequence so that we can easily locate the first outfits to be worn upon reaching our first destination. The packing has to be handled meticulously to ensure that no creasing or damage occurs. Hats go into large hat boxes packed with tissue to keep the crown of the hat in shape, and with more tissue to protect the trimmings from moving or becoming damaged.

Once all the packing has been completed and the luggage clearly labelled, it is all collected for transportation by the Logistics Team. The same is true on the return journey when all the luggage is delivered back to the Dressers' Floor. It really is like a military operation – and it pays to be well prepared.

Working with jewellery

I̶T IS a great honour and privilege to be entrusted with the care of The Queen's private jewellery and to help select the items that are worn on a daily basis. Again, the final choice is always made by The Queen, but based on a selection that I will have made to complement the outfit she will be wearing and appropriate for the occasion.

For state occasions, a tiara is always required. The Vladimir Tiara (pictured) was purchased by Queen Mary in 1921 from the collection of the Grand Duchess Vladimir, aunt of Tsar Nicholas II, for whom it was made in the 1870s.

It is the most complex piece of jewellery in the collection and is made up of fifteen intertwined diamond-set ovals from which hang pendant pearls. The pearls can be interchanged with emeralds and The Queen has worn the tiara with both arrangements during her reign, and sometimes with neither.

The pearls and emeralds are kept in numbered pouches to signify their position on the tiara and it takes nearly an hour to change them over. The changeover of the pearls to emeralds requires a firm grip to get each jewel securely hooked into place. You will notice that I am not wearing gloves when handling the jewellery: this allows me to take secure hold of all the pieces. I always ensure that I take my time to do this quietly and without interruption, as you cannot afford to put the jewels in the wrong pouches or the wrong places on the tiara.

Jewellery for state and style

THE QUEEN has an impressive collection of jewellery in a range of coloured stones, such as the Burmese ruby tiara shown here – which was made for Her Majesty in 1973 – so that for a state visit or a royal tour overseas we can usually find exactly the right colour combination to suit the national colours of the country concerned. Rubies always go well with white outfits, but would never be worn with an orange or red gown: they will clash with orange and disappear with red.

For a state banquet The Queen often wears an order from the country that she is visiting or the country whose Head of State is visiting her, and the colour of that decoration will also determine the colour of the gown to be worn.

Diamonds that dance with light

DIAMONDS are very versatile, because their rainbow-coloured flashes of light complement outfits of any colour, pale as well as stronger ones. The shape and depth of the neckline of an outfit will determine the length of the necklace to be worn. The Queen has some magnificent jewellery, including the examples shown here, which might be familiar to you because she often wears them on formal occasions and overseas state visits. The Queen prefers to wear one necklace at a time, unlike her grandmother, Queen Mary, who was in the habit of wearing multiple pieces.

Look carefully: can you see in the shadows a row
of little girls of Great Britain and Ireland holding hands?

The Queen is very fond of the 'Girls of Great Britain and Ireland' tiara, which was given to her grandmother, Queen Mary, on her marriage in 1893, and that was in turn given to The Queen as a wedding present. The Queen wears the tiara frequently, as it is the lightest of all the tiaras, and it is shown in her portrait on some coins and banknotes.

Calming aquamarine

AQUAMARINES are very majestic in appearance but look cool and calming and are best worn with pale summer colours, especially white and pastel blues and pinks. The inclusion of diamonds helps to define the solid colour of the aquamarines.

The necklace and matching pair of earrings opposite were given to The Queen by the President and People of Brazil for her Coronation in 1953. The original pendant from the necklace was subsequently mounted as the centrepiece of a new matching tiara, shown below, and replaced by a smaller stone. The tiara was made for The Queen in 1957. Originally simpler in form, it was adapted in 1971 by the addition of the four scroll ornaments from an aquamarine presented by the Governor of São Paolo in 1968.

A sea of pearls

THE PEARLS on these two pages are also from The Queen's private jewellery collection and are worn on less formal occasions such as private dinners and when a dance is being held. The more elaborate arrangements of pearls interspersed with diamonds are the ones that The Queen likes to wear on state or grander occasions.

Presenting the jewellery

THE UPKEEP of the jewellery involves regular cleaning and maintenance. Depending on how many times an item is worn, it may also require a deep clean. When cleaning the jewellery, I will wear my white cotton gloves and use a soft jeweller's cloth. This also gives me the opportunity to check for loose stones and fixings, scratches or other concerns. If repairs or deep cleaning are necessary, I will then schedule a date for The Queen's private jewellers to come to Buckingham Palace to undertake the work under my supervision.

The trays that we use for presenting jewellery to The Queen are themselves a little bit special: they once belonged to The Queen's grandmother, Queen Mary. The lace covers were handsewn by Queen Mary herself and bear her own 'M' monogram. We also use lace handkerchiefs when presenting a selection of brooches and hat pins for The Queen to make her choice. We usually lay out three brooches that we think will work well with the outfit she is wearing. The Queen makes her own choice, pins the brooch on to her coat herself, and then is ready to go.

The 2012 Diamond Jubilee

Her Majesty The Queen took part in an exhilarating range of wonderful events during her extended Jubilee programme from March to July, with the highlight being the Diamond Jubilee weekend in June.

The following pages detail the outfits chosen by Her Majesty to wear during some of the regional visits and the main Diamond Jubilee weekend.

Out and about

1 March 2012
London

8 March 2012
Leicester

23 March 2012
Greater Manchester

26 ~ 27 April 2012

Wales

2 May 2012

Somerset and Devon

9 ~ 13 May 2012

*Royal Windsor
Horse Show*

18 May 2012

*Sovereigns' Lunch,
Windsor Castle*

A summer to remember

19 May 2012
Armed Forces Muster,
Windsor Castle

3 June 2012
Thames Diamond
Jubilee Pageant

4 June 2012
Diamond Jubilee Concert,
Buckingham Palace

5 June 2012
Service of Thanksgiving,
St Paul's Cathedral

19 ~ 23 June 2012	26 June 2012	27 June 2012	27 July 2012
Royal Ascot	*Enniskillen, Northern Ireland*	*Belfast, Northern Ireland*	*Opening of the London Olympics*

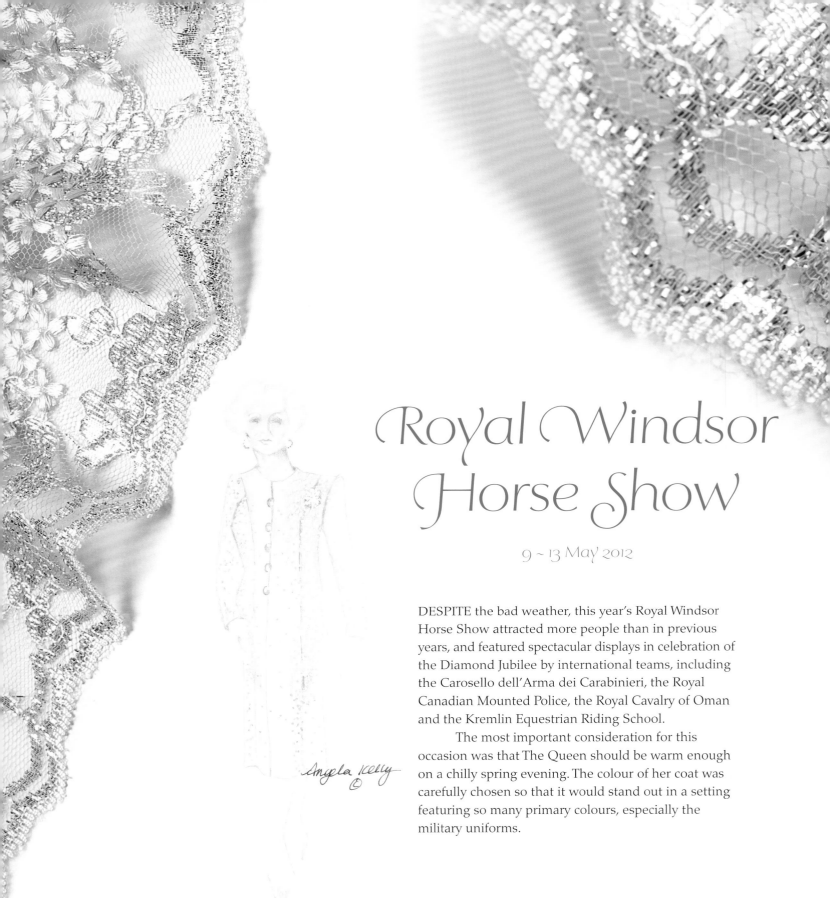

Royal Windsor Horse Show

9 ~ 13 May 2012

Angela Kelly ©

DESPITE the bad weather, this year's Royal Windsor Horse Show attracted more people than in previous years, and featured spectacular displays in celebration of the Diamond Jubilee by international teams, including the Carosello dell'Arma dei Carabinieri, the Royal Canadian Mounted Police, the Royal Cavalry of Oman and the Kremlin Equestrian Riding School.

The most important consideration for this occasion was that The Queen should be warm enough on a chilly spring evening. The colour of her coat was carefully chosen so that it would stand out in a setting featuring so many primary colours, especially the military uniforms.

Sovereigns' Lunch
Windsor Castle
18 May 2012

Angela Kelly ©

THE QUEEN and The Duke of Edinburgh welcomed twenty-five sovereign monarchs from around the world to Windsor Castle to celebrate the Diamond Jubilee. Other members of the British Royal Family also attended, including The Duke and Duchess of Cambridge, Prince Harry, The Duke of York and Princesses Beatrice and Eugenie, and The Earl and Countess of Wessex.

A reception was held in the Waterloo Chamber before lunch was served in St George's Hall. Afterwards, the guests visited the Royal Library and State Apartments to see treasures from the Royal Collection. The Queen's outfit, in the form of a classic 'box jacket', featured hand-embroidery with beads reused from an earlier garment.

*The Queen meeting her
guests at the lunch for
sovereign monarchs
held at Windsor Castle*

Armed Forces Muster
Windsor Castle
19 May 2012

MORE than 2,500 troops led by six massed bands paraded before The Queen and The Duke of Edinburgh in a spectacular Armed Forces Diamond Jubilee tribute at Windsor. The Queen and The Duke of Edinburgh watched from a dais in the Quadrangle as the parade began with a fly-past of RAF Typhoons in the Diamond Nine formation.

For this thrilling occasion, which The Queen visibly enjoyed, I wanted to try something new. Although The Queen appeared to be wearing an open-fronted coat, a panel in the same fabric as the dress worn underneath was attached on either side of the coat, to prevent it from opening in the strong breeze.

Notice the detail on the cuffs and crown of the hat: it was especially pleated for Her Majesty.

Thames River Pageant

3 June 2012

THE MOST spectacular event of the Diamond Jubilee celebrations took place on London's river, where a thousand vessels proceeded from Battersea to Tower Bridge. Tens of thousands of wellwishers lined the banks of the Thames to see one of the largest flotillas ever assembled on the river, with rowed boats, working boats and pleasure vessels of all shapes and sizes beautifully dressed and turned out in their finest rigs.

The Queen travelled in the *Spirit of Chartwell*, which was magnificently decorated with gilded carvings and ten thousand flowers. As the last vessels approached Tower Bridge the weather deteriorated but the London Philharmonic Orchestra and the Royal College of Music Chamber Choir continued their programme of patriotic music to the bitter end. The Pageant day was also the public launch of the Queen Elizabeth Diamond Jubilee Trust, which aims to raise funds for good causes in the UK and the Commonwealth – with a particular focus on young people.

The old dressmakers' stands are the best!

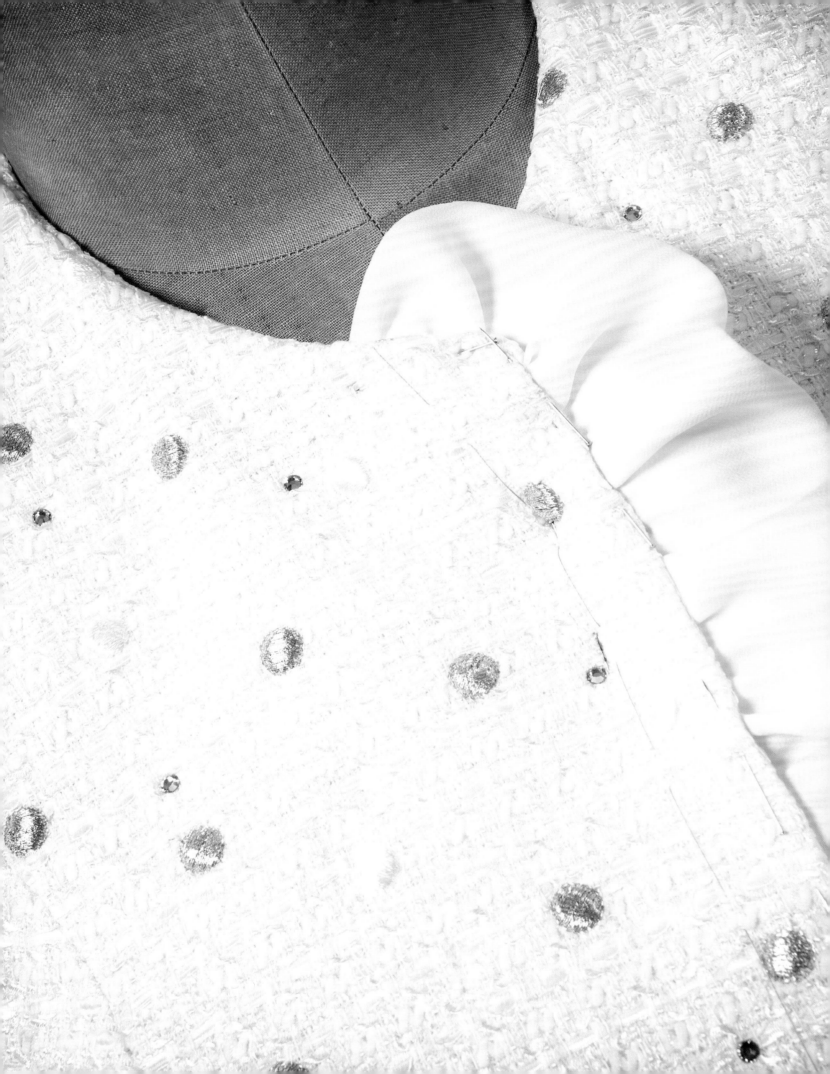

This was a unique occasion of a kind not seen since Tudor times, and we began planning this outfit almost two years ahead of the event. I thought about the sort of costumes that Queen Elizabeth I used to wear, which were often richly jewelled on a white background. White was also important because I knew that on board the barge The Queen would be surrounded by strong reds in the carpets, upholstery and canopy. We never imagined that the weather would turn out so badly, but I am glad that we gave The Queen some protection from the wind and rain with the frill that ran round the coat's neckline and down its front, and the matching white cashmere pashmina. The overall effect suggested Britannia, the ruler of a maritime nation.

Diamond Jubilee Concert

4 June 2012

THIS HISTORIC concert, a celebration of The Queen's sixty-year reign through music, took place on a specially constructed stage surrounding the Queen Victoria Memorial, with Buckingham Palace as the backdrop.

Ten thousand members of the public won a nationwide ballot for tickets to the concert, preceded by a picnic in the garden of the Palace.

Blessed for once with fine weather throughout the occasion, the evening featured a programme of British music from the six decades of Her Majesty's reign.

The fact that The Queen was appearing on stage at a concert suggested a theatrical mood. For those of us working in Buckingham Palace the Queen Victoria Memorial is a familiar friend and it was the golden figure on top of the monument that gave me the idea for the colour of The Queen's dress. The monument was transformed into a circular stage for the concert. While the music reflected every decade of Her Majesty's reign, I wonder how many people realised that the fabric of The Queen's gown was itself a period piece – bought overseas as long ago as 1961. This was not a state occasion so there was to be no jewellery, which in any case would not be right for a pop concert. Nor was it necessary, given the extravagant embroidered appliqué running over one shoulder of the dress. You may have noticed that at an earlier stage we had put it on the opposite shoulder; it was The Queen's decision to change it round, and absolutely right that we did.

Service of Thanksgiving
St Paul's Cathedral

5 June 2012

ON THE morning following the Jubilee Concert The Queen and other
members of the Royal Family took part in a Service of Thanksgiving
for Her Majesty's service over sixty years. Whereas the previous
two days were all about spectacle, huge crowds and outdoor events,
the mood for St Paul's needed to be calm and serene yet supremely
elegant. The dress, with self-covered buttons, was accompanied by
a pale chiffon scarf, draped and stitched down on the left shoulder.
The Queen chose to wear the 'Cullinan III and IV' diamond brooch,
a very simple yet unmistakable reference to the Diamond Jubilee.

Royal Ascot

19 ~ 23 June 2012

ASCOT is one of the long-standing fixtures of
The Queen's year and calls for different, but
not necessarily new, outfits on each of the race
days. This pink ensemble featured hand-made
rouleaux, or small rolls of fabric (seen here on the
left), made up into bows on the bell sleeves.

On the Friday The Queen's own filly,
Estimate, won the Queen's Vase Stakes.
The presentation of the trophy to the winning
owner by The Duke of Edinburgh was an
unforgettable moment of the Diamond
Jubilee season.

Angela Kelly MVO

Northern Ireland

THE QUEEN wore a green outfit for her arrival last year in the Republic of Ireland on the first day of her historic state visit. To ring the changes for the latest of Her Majesty's visits to Northern Ireland, we chose the peaceful colours and elegant lines of this 'Wedgwood' look. Any visit to the Emerald Isle has to feature green at some stage, so for the second day we chose a lime fabric, softened by gold lace, with a new style of collar. This was what The Queen was wearing for the widely reported meeting with Deputy First Minister Martin McGuinness, who himself wore a pale green tie.

The London* 2012 Olympics

27 July ~ 12 August 2012

'Good evening, Mr Bond'

THE LONDON 2012 Olympics Opening Ceremony was an event full of colour, sound, dance, light and movement, with thousands of volunteers creating choreographed patterns across the huge floor of the Olympic stadium. But amidst this kaleidoscope of colour and activity, there was one moment of hushed concentration, as 62,000 people in the Olympic stadium and a billion TV viewers around the world watched the screens in amazement as James Bond arrived at Buckingham Palace, to be greeted by corgis Monty,

Willow and Holly and then by The Queen with the famous words: 'Good evening, Mr Bond'.

Flying by helicopter over the Houses of Parliament, saluted by Winston Churchill's statue in Westminster Square, passing beneath Tower Bridge and swinging north to Stratford and the Olympic Stadium, Mr Bond and The Queen prepared their next daring move: the helicopter door slid open and The Queen, dressed in a crystal and lace peach beaded cocktail dress, apparently took a daring leap, skydiving towards the stadium from 500 feet.

Why two dresses?

On Her Majesty's Secret Service

THIS DRAMATIC moment, when the whole world was held in a state of suspense, wondering whether The Queen had safely executed her dramatic entry into the Olympic arena, was followed by thunderous applause and a standing ovation as Her Majesty walked calmly and unruffled to her place, accompanied by The Duke of Edinburgh and Jacques Rogge, President of the International Olympic Committee.

The whole show-stopping moment was dependent on that dress – the visual clue to the identity of the figure first glimpsed on film, seated at her desk in Buckingham Palace, then walking purposefully along the red carpet to the waiting helicopter, before descending decorously beneath a parachute of red, white and blue towards the stadium to open the 2012 Olympic Games.

Dress 1

Angola Kelly MVO.

Dress 2

Angola Kelly MVO.

Keeping it under wraps

NEEDLESS TO SAY, months of preparation went into the planning of this key moment when, instead of arriving predictably by carriage or car, The Queen seemingly abandoned protocol to accompany Mr Bond on his parachute jump.

The key to its success was the making of two identical versions of the same dress (one for the stunt double), to give the illusion that Her Majesty was actually jumping from the helicopter. I worked closely with Danny Boyle's team and the Olympic Opening Ceremony costume department to achieve this effect. The sequence, presented in a short film 'Happy and Glorious', was a closely guarded secret until the last moment. Even Her Majesty's family was surprised. The Buckingham Palace dressmakers worked quietly for months, never having both dresses out of storage at the same time – even they did not know why two dresses were required for the same event.

The colour of the dress was also fundamental to the success of the sequence. We needed a solid colour that would stand out when The Queen descended towards the giant stadium, and within the setting of the stadium itself, which was a sea of colours. At the same time, care needed to be taken to choose a colour that was not associated strongly with any of the participating Olympic nations. Another important feature of the dress was its pleated skirt, which had to be identifiable as The Queen left the Palace so that it would be recognised as she descended from the helicopter, creating a visual sequence.

The Queen wore a headpiece carefully designed by me and made by Stella in the workshop at Buckingham Palace from ostrich feathers, dyed the same colour as the dress and decorated with the same floral clusters of petals, sequins and glass beads.

After all the excitement of The Queen's arrival at the Opening Ceremony, it was time for a more reflective moment as the Union Flag was raised by members of Her Majesty's Armed Forces, while the first and third verses of the national anthem were performed by members of the Kaos Signing Choir for Deaf and Hearing Children. Later in the ceremony, just after midnight in the United Kingdom, The Queen declared the Olympic Games open, followed by a short but stunning firework display that could be heard all over London.

The Queen returned to the Olympic Park the next day to meet athletes and dignitaries. The Opening Ceremony was a spectacular start to an extraordinarily successful Olympic Games – and The Queen's part in it will surely be remembered forever as a quintessentially British moment.

And that's how
to do a Jubilee

Off to Balmoral ...

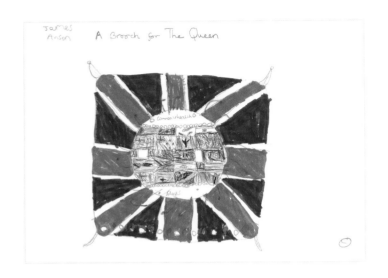

James Anson — A Brooch for The Queen

This dress is for wearing in Windsor somtims

by Scarlett Elisabeth Anson

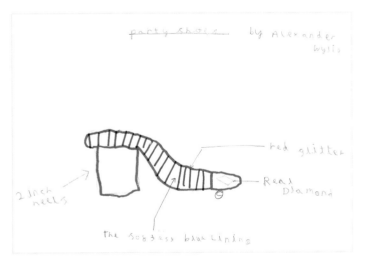

party shoes by Alexander Wylie

2 inch heels

red glitter

Real Diamond

The softest blue Lining

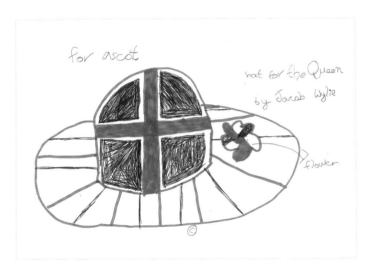

for ascot

hat for the Queen by Jacob Wylie

flower

Keeping it in the family: future designers

Acknowledgements

WORKING at Buckingham Palace has been such an honour and privilege with great excitement that I have not noticed the last eighteen years passing by. I never thought in my lifetime that I would write a book, let alone a book about Her Majesty The Queen; the moment I was given permission, I had a vision of how the story should be told.

Your Majesty, from the bottom of my heart, I am truly thankful.

Most importantly, I thank my family, who continue to support me and understand fully the responsibilities I have within my role as Personal Assistant to Her Majesty The Queen. Their continued love and reassurance is so much appreciated. This is my opportunity to let the whole world know how much I love them.

The year of the Diamond Jubilee and the preparations involved is a good reflection of my work involving part of the private and public life of The Queen. Without a doubt, it is full of excitement, intrigue, hard work but above all loyalty and discretion. Writing a book during the production of a Diamond Jubilee couture collection was always going to be quite a challenge. However, I have never been shy of hard work or being faced with a mountain to climb, but it is the people around me that I really must praise and thank for all their concern and support over the years, not just this busy year.

Many thanks go to the Director of the Royal Collection, Jonathan Marsden, for keeping me on the straight and narrow; his expertise has guided and helped me to achieve this wonderful book. Jonathan: thank you.

Also I am so grateful for the guidance and advice I received from: Sir Christopher Geidt, who gave permission for me to write this book and believed that I was capable of making it a success; Samantha Cohen who has worked so hard and who has been a joy to work alongside whilst helping to make this book a success; Sir Alan Reid for not only being my mentor but for many years of his valuable support and advice; all The Queen's Ladies in Waiting, for their friendship and guidance; Mr Edward Young for believing this book was going to be a great success and all his enthusiastic support; Colonel Andrew Ford for encouraging me and never doubting that I could write this book; and Ailsa Anderson who has always believed in me.

Mostly my gratitude goes to Rianna Sullivan who has worked tirelessly with me to produce the endless pages of text; she continued to complete her own work alongside the extra workload and managed to keep smiling through it all.

The Queen's dressers and the dressmaking team on the Dressers' Floor have been amazing whilst creating this book and documenting every aspect of our work, which is normally kept very private and therefore I am grateful for their ability to maintain the same privacy and discretion.

I would also like to thank The Queen's Pages, Paul Whybrew and Barry Mitford, for their professionalism, discretion, loyalty and friendship they both share with all of us, it means so much to me and working alongside them is a great privilege. The Queen's Footmen, Ian Robinson and William Barras, apart from their own duties, also assist us on the Dressers' Floor with the luggage, and we appreciate all that they do.

My thanks and gratitude must also go to Mark Nelson, who I knew would be an endless support for me as a friend and colleague. Mark was able to bring his business management skills to plan the creative elements of the book and structure a project. Mark's patience in helping me write the book was beyond anything anyone could ask for, his constant support and long emails regardless what time of the day or night! His loyalty, friendship and determination to get it right for me astounded me at times; he never gave up, even when I was so tired he kept me going and I truly thank you for that Mark. I must also thank Bernard Connolly for his beautiful illustrations of my designs and also for setting the stage for the photographs. I want to thank him for his loyalty and friendship.

Also, I would like to say thank you to Barry Jeffery for taking the wonderful photographs, to Eva Zielinska-Millar, for her time and creativity in photographing Her Majesty's private jewellery, and to Ray Watkins for the beautiful layout of the pages.

And to Annie Miles for her guidance, enthusiasm, advice and copy editing skills at the very beginning, which helped me greatly. Finally, to my dear and close friend, Annette Wilkin: thank you for all your kindness and support over many years; you are a true friend. And to my friends Karl Dunkley, Juan Credidio and Stanley Tucker, a big thank you; it means so much to me knowing that you are always there for me.

First published 2012, reprinted 2012

Find out more about the Royal Collection at www.royalcollection.org.uk

ISBN 978 1 905686 74 2

British Library Cataloguing in Publication Data:
A catalogue record for this book is available from the British Library

014284

Project Manager and Editor: Kate Owen
Fashion Photography: Barry Jeffery
Jewellery Photography: Eva Zielinska-Millar
Fashion Illustrations: Bernard Connolly
Book Design: Price Watkins
Book Production: Debbie Wayment

Typeset in Palatino, Young Finesse and Schneidler Initials
Printed on Claro Silk 170gsm
Colour reproduction by Altaimage, London
Printed and bound in the UK by Butler Tanner and Dennis Ltd

ILLUSTRATIONS

Unless otherwise stated, all illustrations are © HM Queen Elizabeth II 2012.
Royal Collection Trust is grateful for permission to reproduce the items
listed below:

Camera Press: p. 28
**Crown © Photographer: Sergeant S L Hughes RLC, Media Operations
London District:** p. 98 (right)
Getty: pp. 10–11; 98 (centre right); 124 (left); 128 (top); 130–1; 133 (bottom
centre); 134 (inset); 138
© 2012 International Olympic Committee: p. 133 (top, bottom left and
bottom right)
PA: pp. 9; 44; 45; 48 (top and bottom); 60; 62–3 (all except p. 63, top row,
right); 69; 71; 94; 95; 96 (all); 97 (centre left, centre right and right); 98 (left
and centre left); 99 (all); 101; 103 (both); 108 (both); 109; 110 (inset); 112
(inset); 113; 114–15; 116; 118–19; 119 (inset); 122 (both); 125; 126 (top); 127
(both); 128 (bottom); 129; 134–5; 139
Reuters: p. 97 (left)
Rex Features: pp. 63 (top row, right); 123